# GREAT WHITE SHARK

## BY ROBIN TWIDDY

**BookLife**
PUBLISHING

©2019
**BookLife Publishing**
**King's Lynn**
**Norfolk PE30 4LS**

All rights reserved.
Printed in Malaysia.

A catalogue record for this
book is available from the
British Library.

**ISBN:** 978-1-78637-611-4

Written by:
Robin Twiddy

Edited by:
Kirsty Holmes

Designed by:
Danielle Rippengill

# IMAGE CREDITS

All images are courtesy of Shutterstock.com, unless otherwise specified. With thanks to Getty Images, Thinkstock Photo and iStockphoto.
Cover – Martin Prochazkacz, Ivan Kurmyshov, Andrey_Kuzmin, arka38. Boarder used throughout – arka38. Background Images –
Ivan Kurmyshov, Andrey_Kuzmin, Song Heming, pirke, vovan. 2 – wildestanimal. 4 – Sergey Uryadnikov. 5 – Stefan Pircher. 6 – Martin
Prochazkacz. 7 – SSaplaima. 8 & 9 – Tomas Kotouc. 10 – Alexyz3d. 11 – Masini. 12 – Alessandro De Maddalena. 13 – Alexius Sutandio.
14 – Palomba. 15 – Alessandro De Maddalena. 16 – Shane Gross, Marc Henauer. 17 – wildestanimal. 18 – Sergey Uryadnikov.
19 – VisionDive. 20 – VisionDive, Petr Jilek, Ondrej Prosicky, Shane Myers Photography. 21 – Mogens Trolle. 22 – Elsa Hoffmann.
23 – solarseven.

# CONTENTS

WORDS THAT LOOK LIKE <u>this</u> CAN BE FOUND IN THE GLOSSARY ON PAGE 24.

# THE GREAT WHITE

There are around 440 known species of shark. Some are small, and some are large. Sharks have **evolved** for millions of years to be the **apex predators** of the ocean.

There is only one species of great white shark. They can be found near to the coast, in waters that are between 12 and 24°C.

BITING FACTS:
THE GREAT WHITE'S SCIENTIFIC NAME IS CARCHARODON CARCHARIAS. THIS ROUGHLY MEANS JAGGED TOOTH!

The females are usually larger than the males and can grow up to 6.1 metres (m) long. Males usually grow to around 4.0 m long.

# TEETH

The great white shark has around five rows of teeth.

BITING FACTS:
THE GREAT WHITE, LIKE OTHER SHARKS, CAN LOSE AND REPLACE AROUND 30,000 TEETH IN ITS LIFETIME!

The front row are larger and used to bite **prey**. The teeth are large, triangular and **serrated**. This means that when they bite, the teeth cut through flesh like a saw!

The teeth in the great white shark's mouth move like a **conveyor belt**. When one tooth is lost at the front, the ones behind move forward to replace it!

# NOSE

Great white shark nostrils, called nares, are not used for breathing. They are only for smelling.

BITING FACTS:
IF THE GREAT WHITE SHARK IS TICKLED ON THE NOSE, IT IS SENT INTO A <u>TRANCE</u>!

However, this shark can smell well enough to detect a group of seals up to 3.2 kilometres away!

Like most sharks, when the great white swims along, water moves through the nostrils. This allows it to detect blood and other things from its prey.

**BITING FACTS:**
THE GREAT WHITE SHARK'S NOSE IS VERY POINTED LIKE A CONE. THIS HELPS IT MOVE THROUGH THE WATER.

# SKELETON

Shark skeletons are not made of bone like land animals' skeletons. Their skeletons are made of **cartilage**. It is lighter and more flexible than bone, allowing the shark to float more easily.

**BITING FACTS:**
BECAUSE SHARKS DO NOT HAVE RIBS, THEY CAN BE CRUSHED UNDER THEIR OWN WEIGHT WHEN OUT OF THE WATER.

BITING FACTS:
SHARKS HAVE SUPPORTING RODS MADE OUT OF CARTILAGE IN THEIR FINS.

Cartilage isn't as strong as bone. So where sharks need extra strength, such as in the jaw and the spine, there is extra **calcium** to make the cartilage stronger.

# EYES

All sharks have great vision and can see really well in dark or murky water. Different types of shark have different eyes, **adapted** to how deep in the ocean they live.

**BITING FACTS:**
GREAT WHITE SHARK
EYES LOOK BLACK BUT
THEY ARE ACTUALLY
A VERY DARK BLUE!

The deeper the shark lives, the smaller its eyes will be.

Part of the eye, called the retina, is divided into two parts. One is for seeing in normal daylight. The other is for seeing in low light.

BITING FACTS:
THE GREAT WHITE WILL ROLL ITS EYES BACK INTO ITS HEAD TO PROTECT THEM WHEN FEEDING.

This means the shark can be a deadly hunter all the time!

# FINS

All sharks have either four or five types of fin.
The great white shark has five types of fin. These are:

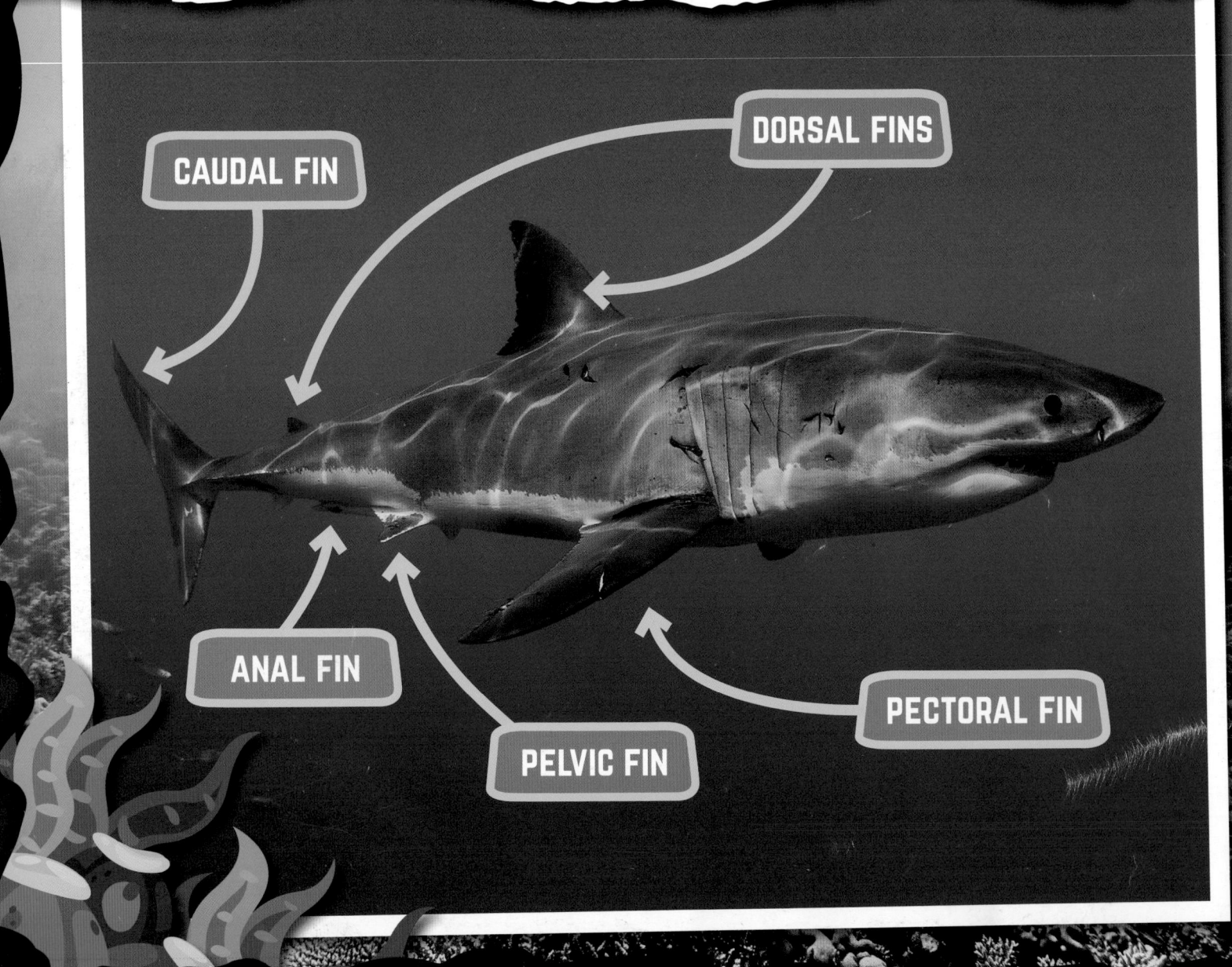

CAUDAL FIN

DORSAL FINS

ANAL FIN

PELVIC FIN

PECTORAL FIN

The different fins have different jobs when it comes to keeping the shark upright in the water and for swimming. When a great white drops its pectoral fins, it is getting ready to move quickly.

# SKIN

Shark skin is covered in tiny, tooth-like scales, called dermal denticles. The way that these are layered forces water past them, making the shark quick in the water.

BITING FACTS:
SHARK SKIN IS ROUGH LIKE SANDPAPER!

DERMAL DENTICLES

A great white shark's skin can range from grey to brown or blue on its dorsal side (the top of the shark).

BITING FACTS:
THESE COLOURS CAMOUFLAGE THE GREAT WHITE AGAINST THE LIGHT SURFACE OR DARK DEPTHS OF THE OCEAN.

The bright white on its ventral side (the underside of the shark) is where it gets its name.

# TAIL

The tail fin is called the caudal fin. This is the fin that the shark uses to speed up and slow down. The great white shark's caudal fin is roughly the same length at the top and the bottom.

The great white uses its powerful tail to **propel** itself through the water, by moving it from side to side. The even, **crescent**-shaped caudal fin allows the shark a lot of control over its movement.

# FOOD CHAIN

Food chains show us which animals eat each other. The great white shark is at the top of its food chain. This means that it is an apex predator.

The great white will eat smaller fish (including smaller sharks), dolphins, porpoises, whales, seals, sea turtles and sea birds.

Sharks have special organs called the ampullae of Lorenzini which pick up electrical signals. The great white shark's are so powerful that they can pick up the electric signal of a heartbeat!

SMALL OPENINGS (PORES) OF THE AMPULLAE OF LORENZINI

BITING FACTS:
ELECTRICAL SIGNALS MAKE THE HEART BEAT.

# LIFE CYCLE

The great white shark is ovoviviparous (say: oh-vo-vi-vi-par-us).

This means that the babies grow inside an egg, but then hatch whilst still inside the mother. This takes about 11 months.

Baby sharks, called pups, are usually born in a litter of two to ten. The pups must look after themselves without their mother's help.

**BITING FACTS:**
GREAT WHITE PUPS ARE QUITE LARGE WHEN THEY ARE BORN, MEASURING ABOUT 1.5 METRES.

Males are fully mature and can breed at the age of nine or ten, whilst females mature at ages of around 14 to 16.

# GLOSSARY

**ADAPTED** — changed over time to suit the environment

**APEX PREDATORS** — animals that are at the top of the food chain and are not prey for another animal

**CALCIUM** — a substance that is used by the body to build healthy bones and teeth

**CAMOUFLAGE** — traits that allow an animal to hide itself in a habitat

**CARTILAGE** — a flexible tissue that acts like bone in cartilaginous fish such as sharks

**CONVEYOR BELT** — a machine to move items on a mechanical belt

**CRESCENT** — a curved, semi-circle shape that the moon sometimes takes

**EVOLVED** — developed over a long time to become adapted to a certain habitat

**PREY** — animals that are hunted by other animals for food

**PROPEL** — to be moved forward by a force

**SERRATED** — to have small notches or teeth like a saw that help to cut

**TRANCE** — a state that seems to be between being asleep and awake

# INDEX